Romantic Mischief

Gregory J.P. Godek

bestselling author of *1001 Ways to Be Romantic*

CASABLANCA PRESS
A DIVISION OF SOURCEBOOKS
NAPERVILLE, IL

Published by: Sourcebooks, Inc.
P.O. Box 372, Naperville, Illinois 60566
(630) 961-3900
FAX: (630) 961-2168

Cover design by Scott Theisen
Internal design and production by Andrew Sardina, Scott Theisen
and Joe Leamon

$\mathscr{D}$edication

To the mischievous lovers and playful romantics of the world.

And, of course, to my Bride, Tracey—my playmate for life.

Library of Congress Cataloging-in-Publication Data
Godek, Gregory J.P.
        Romantic mischief / by Gregory J.P. Godek
                p.   cm. — (A Casablanca book)
            ISBN 1-57071-151-8 (pbk.)
            1. Man-woman relationships — Miscellanea.   2. Love —Miscellanea.   I.
Title.   II. Series.
HQ801.G564 1997
306.7 — dc21   96-49960
                                                                             CIP

Contents

Introduction

$\mathcal{C}$upid would love this book! It's full of fun and mischief, just like he was. Cupid—the personification of romantic love—was a mischievous youth, not a serious adult. Too many of us see love as work, and overanalyze our relationships.

Love should be fun—and this book will help re-introduce you to the playful side of love. It will do so in hundreds of specific and practical ways. Some of them are kinda crazy and somewhat unusual, but you're sure to find lots of ideas that will strike your fancy.

A sense of playfulness goes a long way in helping us keep our love alive. Your playfulness is inborn, and your creativity is far greater than you probably think. This book is designed to help you play more by giving you ideas and sparking your imagination.

I have gathered many new ideas and proven concepts—from the *1001 Ways To Be Romantic* series of books, from my seminars and from my readers—

all designed to inspire you and remind you that love should be fun!

I invite you to keep this book handy or hidden away, and use it as a romantic secret weapon for when you've temporarily run out of ideas.

Gregory J.P. Godek
January 1997

The Weird and Wacky

1

*W*rite "I LOVE YOU" on the bathroom mirror with a piece of soap.

2

*E*at dinner by candlelight. Heck—eat breakfast by candlelight!

3

*L*ove is timeless—and to prove it, cover-up all the clocks in your house for the entire weekend.

Romance resides in the everyday.

*L*earn to say "I love you" in Japanese ("Ai shite imasu"); in Russian ("Ya lyublyu tyebya"); in Eskimo ("Nagligivaget").

Happy Valentine's Day

*I*nstead of actually being romantic on Valentine's Day, why don't you use the day as a chance to re-dedicate yourself to the ideals of love? Make a Valentine's Day Resolution.

You could resolve to call her more often. Be more considerate of him. Listen to her better. Give him more of your time. Stop making excuses. Reserve weekends for each other.

2

Send a dozen roses. Make sure there are eleven red roses and one white rose. Here's the note: "In every bunch there's one who stands out. And you are that one."

3

Buy piles of those little candy conversation hearts. Fill the sink with them. Fill his briefcase, fill her purse. Fill her favorite cereal box with them.

4

Send fourteen Valentine's Day cards: one-a-day starting February 1st.

5

On Valentine's Day, give your partner one card every hour.

Romance 101

1

*C*all your lover every hour on the hour...all day long!...just to say "I love you."

2

*D*on't bother with a dozen roses...one is plenty! But make sure you attach a personal and heartfelt note. Maybe the lyrics to his or her favorite love song.

3

*S*ave the little slips of paper from Hershey's Kisses. Give them to your partner along with a note that says, "These are Love Coupons—each one is redeemable for one kiss."

Romantic Mischief

ᶴome romantic inscriptions for notes, gifts and
jewelry:

- ✤ A.A.F. (Always And Forever)
- ✤ G.M.F.L. (Geese Mate For Life)
- ✤ A.T.S.B.O. (And They Shall Be One)
- ✤ T.L.Y.T.I.E.T.T.L.Y.M. (Ask a Beatles fan. Hint:
  From Abbey Road)

Spontaneous Combustion

𝒜nd then there are some romantic situations
that are impossible to plan:

- ✤ Seeing a falling star streak across the sky—and
  making a romantic wish on it together.
- ✤ Finding beautiful wildflowers while on a walk.

- Catching a rainbow.

- Stumbling upon a great little romantic restaurant.

- Finding a secluded spot to make love.

- Discovering a great little bed-and-breakfast while traveling.

2

"*A*-to-Z Romantic Exclamations": Write a series of 26 "romantic thoughts" to your partner. Begin each one with a word that starts with a different letter of the alphabet:

- A—Always and forever—that's how long I'll love you!

- B—Be my one-and-only!

- C—Come closer, my honey bun!

3

Send a taxi to pick him up after work; pre-pay the cab fare (including tip!) and instruct the driver to take him to your favorite restaurant, where you'll be waiting for him!

4

One romantic fellow writes a poem every year to celebrate the events, accomplishments and funny things that he and his wife share. He's got 23 years worth of poems!

Surprise!

1

The different types of romantic surprises:

- Total surprises
- Unfolding surprises
- Bait-and-switch surprises

- Mystery event surprises
- Big surprises
- Little surprises
- Once-in-a-lifetime surprises
- Expected but-not-right-now surprises
- Group surprises
- Surprise vacations
- Surprises in public
- Surprises in private
- Surprises involving one or more collaborators

2

Chinese fortune cookies with custom fortunes
that you write and slip inside!

3

*D*oes he read his horoscope every day in the newspaper? Get the paper before he does. Write a custom horoscope (funny, sexy or just plain outrageous!) and paste it over his real one.

4

*G*reet him a the door with confetti.

Romantic Strategies

1

*B*e just 1% more romantic than you currently are. This tiny little 1% will make a 100% difference in your relationship over time. Try it and see.

Romance is about the little things.

2
. . .

*Y*ou don't need to instantly and dramatically become romantic. (Your partner may think you've suddenly gone insane!)

Instead, try this strategy: Make the change slowly...one day at a time...one gesture at a time. You can be a little more romantic, can't you?!

3
. . .

*D*o you want your partner to be more romantic? Set high standards for him or her to live up to! People usually rise or fall to the level of our expectations of them.

Many psychological studies affirm this phenomenon. It's the old "self-fulfilling prophecy" thing.

Be Creative!

1

$\mathscr{M}$ake your own greeting cards. You don't have to be artistic—just heartfelt!

2

$\mathscr{H}$iding places for notes and small gifts: Under the pillow; in the glove compartment; in her briefcase, in his sock drawer, in a pizza box, in the refrigerator.

Become an artist of your relationship.

3

$\mathscr{C}$reate a "Romantic Idea Jar": Write 100 romantic ideas on separate slips of paper. Fill a jar with them. Once a week you take turns picking one idea at random.

$\mathcal{G}$et a journal. Every day, write down your thoughts about your partner, about your relationship, about your lives together.

Some days you'll just jot a quick "I love you"— other days you may be inspired to write for 10 minutes or more. Do this for an entire year. Then present it to him or her on your anniversary or her birthday.

Be Prepared!

1
. . .

$\mathcal{B}$e prepared for spontaneous romantic escapes! Have "His" and "Hers" overnight bags packed at all times. Keep under the bed or in the car trunk.

*B*e prepared for shopping! Know all of your partner's sizes, favorite colors, favorite styles and favorite authors.

———

Great relationships require equal parts of passion, commitment and intimacy.

———

3
. . .

*B*e prepared—for anything! Always have on hand: candles, "Love" stamps, good wine, bubblebath and greeting cards.

4
. . .

*B*e prepared to pop a greeting card in the mail at a moment's notice. Run out and buy $25 worth of cards. Get a mixture of funny, serious. sexv and romantic cards.

*B*e prepared with a library of romantic music.
Include: George Winston's *Autumn*, Natalie Cole's
Unforgettable, Earl Klugh's *Heartstrings*, Enya's
Shepherd Moon.

A Touch of Class

1

*H*ave her portrait painted from a photograph.

2

*H*ire a pianist to play during dinner at home!

Love is not a mystery to be solved...
It is an experience to be savored.

3

Cook a gourmet dinner for two.

4

Propose a toast to her while at a dinner party with friends.

5

Hire a limousine for an elegant evening out.

Gift Ideas

1

"A-to-Z Romantic Gifts": Dedicate yourself to finding one romantic gift or creating one romantic experience for each letter of the alphabet for your partner.

A is for artwork, azaleas, Aretha Franklin albums, antiques

$\mathcal{B}$ is for balloons, books, Beatles albums, Baileys Irish Cream

$\mathcal{C}$ is for chocolate, candles, cards, cookies, CDs, computers, cameras, concerts

$\mathcal{D}$ is for dining out, donuts, diamonds, Dom Perignon

$\mathcal{E}$ is for earrings, escape weekends, engagement rings, erotic movies

$\mathcal{F}$ is for films, flowers, ferris wheel rides, furs, fishing gear, fountain pens

$\mathcal{G}$ is for gemstones, gold, garter belts, gourmet gadgets, guitars, greeting cards

$\mathcal{H}$ is for hats, Hawaiian vacations, honeymoons

$\mathcal{I}$ is for ice cream, Italian vacations, island escapes

$\mathcal{J}$ is for jewelry, jacuzzis, jazz music

$\mathcal{K}$ is for kinky toys, kites, kittens, kiss coupons, Kisses (Hershey's)

$\mathcal{L}$ is for licorice, lingerie, love coupons, luggage, limousine rides, lobster dinners

M is for money, movie tickets, magazine subscriptions, motorcycles

N is for nightgowns, necklaces

O is for opals, ouija board, ornaments, oil lamps

P is for perfume, picnic baskets, popcorn, puppies, poppies, pianos

Q is for quiet, quilts

R is for robes, roses, rings

S is for shoes, satin sheets, satin boxer shorts, socks, spas, sex, skates

T is for T-shirts, tickets, tools, tents, tropical fish, time together

U is for umbrellas, U2 albums

V is for vacations, vases, VCRs

W is for wine, weekend get-aways, watches

X is for X-rated movies, eXtra consideration

Y is for yachts, year-of-romance, Yukon vacation

Z is for zany gifts. (Hey, you try finding a "Z" gift!)

Romantic Strategies

1
. . .

*O*verdo something! Does he like M&M's? Buy him 50 pounds of them! Does she like teddy bears? Get her dozens!

2
. . .

*L*isten! With your ears, mind and heart. Listen for the meaning behind his actions. Listen for the message behind her words.

Time is your most precious commodity. You give yourself when you give your time.

3
. . .

$\mathscr{D}$on't wait for holidays to celebrate...Celebrate because it's Tuesday! Celebrate the new moon. Celebrate your 1,000th day together. Celebrate something every week!

Romantic Classics

1
. . .

$\mathscr{A}$ gold chain and locket—with your picture inside.

2
. . .

$\mathscr{D}$inner at a fine French restaurant.

3
. . .

$\mathscr{T}$he film classic Casablanca.

Commitment requires daily renewal.

4

An evening of dancing and dining.

5

Propose a toast to one another with every glass of wine.

Celebrate!

1

Celebrate the 12 Days of Christmas...The 14 Days of Valentine's Season...The 30 Days Leading to Her Birthday!

2

Have a pair of elegant wine goblets etched with your names or initials.

3

. . .

*C*reate your own "Day-at-a-Time" calendar. The goal is to fill-in every day with events, information and quotes that are unique to the two of you.

4

. . .

*R*un a bubblebath for her. Don't forget the candles. And the rose. And her favorite book. And a little wine.

Of Note

1

. . .

*T*ape a note to your partner's wristwatch: "Time for love!"

2

. . .

*T*ape a note to the TV: "Turn me on instead!"

3

$\mathscr{A}$ homemade greeting card from one spry senior citizen to his wife: "I've fallen in love and I can't get up!"

4

$\mathscr{A}$ttach a note to your partner's calculator: "You can count on me."

Lovers listen with their hearts.

5

$\mathscr{B}$uy a case of wine: Attach a note to each of the 12 bottles:

- ✄ Her birthday
- ✄ His birthday
- ✄ Christmas/Hanukkah

- Our anniversary
- Groundhog Day
- For a midnight snack
- Before making love
- To celebrate a great accomplishment at work
- Mozart's birthday
- The first snowfall of the year
- For making up after a fight
- For the first day of Spring

6

Write 101 little love notes...number them...and hide them all over the house.

7

Buy her a lottery ticket. Attach a note: "You're one in a million!"

Take Note

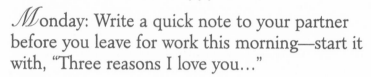

1

Monday: Write a quick note to your partner before you leave for work this morning—start it with, "Three reasons I love you…"

2

Tuesday: Write a quick note to your partner before you leave for work this morning—start it with, "Three things you do that bring a smile to my face…"

3

Wednesday's note: "Three things I'm going to change, because you want me to…"

4

Thursday's note: "Three ideas for romantic get-aways during the next year…"

Romantic Mischief

5

$\mathcal{F}$riday's note: "Three things that first attracted me to you when we first started dating…"

6

$\mathcal{S}$aturday's note: "Three things I'm going to do this weekend to show you how much I love you…"

7

$\mathcal{S}$unday's note: "Three romantic movies that we're going to watch in bed today…"

Unexpected Surprises

1

$\mathcal{A}$rrive home from work with a bottle of wine…and a big smile!

The surprise gift is most appreciated. The unexpected gesture is most treasured.

2

"Sally" has a husband who tinkers with his car incessantly. This used to bother Sally, until she decided to make that car her medium for communicating with hubby.

Her most time-consuming project was a love note attached to the end of the car's oil dipstick! She had a tiny slip of metal engraved with "I love you, Dave! Your Sally" and then carefully wired it to the end of the dipstick. Ol' Dave couldn't believe his squinting eyes!

3

*S*peaking of cars…Another mischievious wife waited for her mechanic husband in the back seat of his car—dressed like a Snap-On Tools calendar girl! (Vroom!)

4

*D*on't give cash as a gift—unless you do it in an unusual or creative way. Well, some of my readers have done just that: They've come up with some ideas that are creative, if not downright unusual!

$ "Long-Stemmed Twenty-Dollar-Bills"

$ "The Hundred-Dollar-Bill Single Rose"

$ "Origami Money"

$ "The Great Toilet Paper Roll of 100 One-Dollar Bills!"

I Love You

1
. . .

*U*pside down stamps on envelopes mean "I love you."

2
. . .

*L*earn how to say "I love you" using sign language. The book *The Joy of Signing*, by Lottie Riekoff, will help!

Romance is the expression of love. It's the "action step"—without which love is merely an empty concept.

3

*F*or your Romance Library: books with "Love" in their titles:

- ✤ *Love is Letting Go of Fear*, by Gerald Jampolsky
- ✤ *Love*, by Leo Buscaglia
- ✤ *The Art of Loving*, by Erich Fromm
- ✤ *Notes on Love and Courage*, by Hugh Prather

4

*P*ut a "JUST MARRIED" sign in your back wind-shield the next time you go for a Sunday afternoon drive…and enjoy the reaction from other drivers!

Love Songs

1

*S*he Describes Infinity, a romantic CD by Scott Cossu.

2
∙∙∙

Down To The Moon, the CD by Andreas
Vollenweider.

3
∙∙∙

A Winter's Solstice, the CD by Windham Hill
artists.

Do's and Don'ts

1
∙∙∙

Guys...don't buy women practical gifts! No toast-
ers, blenders or vacuum cleaners!

2

$\mathcal{D}$o plan ahead. Planning doesn't destroy spontaneity, it creates opportunity.

3

$\mathcal{D}$on't give cash as a gift! (Unless it's really a lot of money!)

4

$\mathcal{D}$on't treat your lover as a stereotype. He's an individual, not a statistic. And she's a unique person, not "just like all women."

5

$\mathcal{D}$o the opposite of what everyone else is doing. Don't go out on New Year's Eve.

Do stay home and cozy-up with your lover near the fireplace.

6

*D*on't buy roses for Valentine's Day.

Do buy flowers that begin with the first letter of her name.

7

*D*on't go to the beach on the crowded weekends.

Do go mid-week.

8

*D*on't give her a birthday present.

Do give her seven gifts—one for each day of her birthday week!

9

*D*on't go shopping for gifts during the crazed Christmas season.

Do shop year-round (and stash those gifts and presents in your Gift Closet).

10

$\mathscr{D}$on't go to popular vacation spots during their most popular seasons.

Do go right on either edge of the hot season.

11

$\mathscr{D}$on't buy show tickets after they're advertised (all the best seats will already be gone).

Do buy a subscription series, become a theatre supporter, or join a "Show-of-the-Month" club.

12

$\mathscr{D}$on't watch your favorite TV shows when they're broadcast (keep control over your own Prime Time).

Do tape them and watch them later.

13

$\mathscr{D}$on't read the newspaper at the breakfast table.

Do talk with one another.

Creative Couples

1

*A*nd then there was the romantic plumber who installed the dual shower head in the shower. (So his honey wouldn't get chilly when they showered together.)

2

*A*nd then there was the romantic farmer who planted a whole field full of roses for his wife. ("Much more romantic than barley," he said.)

3

*A*nd then there was the romantic chef who not only created a gourmet entree to suit his wife's tastes, he named it after her and added it to his restaurant's menu!

*A*nd then there was the guy who wrapped a lingerie gift for his gal inside a heart-shaped box of candy.

5
· · ·

*A*nd then there was the gal who gave her guy a wristwatch. She had the back inscribed with "I always have time for you."

Fun & Games

1
· · ·

*K*idnap him! Blindfold him; drive him around town until he's thoroughly lost; then reveal your destination: his favorite restaurant, the ballpark, or maybe a romantic inn.

2

$\mathcal{H}$ave your handwriting analyzed. Have your astrological charts read. Have your tarot cards read.

Romance is a bridge between the sexes.

3

$\mathcal{E}$very time you stop at a red light, kiss!

4

$\mathcal{G}$ot a few minutes on your hands? Fill his entire answering machine tape with romantic messages, mysterious messages, sexy messages, mischievious messages.

For Men Only

1
. . .

*Y*ou take the kids out for the afternoon…giving her an afternoon of peace and quiet.

2
. . .

*S*have on Saturday night!

Romance is "Adult Play."

3
. . .

A shopping trip for men. Buy one item from each store. Giftwrap each item separately:

- ❧ Crabtree & Evelyn
- ❧ A local liquor store

- Victoria's Secret
- A flower shop
- Hallmark Card Shop
- A jewelry store

4

$\mathscr{D}$o a household chore that's usually one of "her" jobs.

5

$\mathscr{R}$evive chivalry. Open her car door. Hold her dinner chair. Help her on with her coat.

For Women Only

1

$\mathscr{S}$end him a love letter sealed with a kiss. (Use your reddest lipstick.)

2

*S*end flowers to him at work.

3

*D*on't position yourself against his passions. Don't force him to choose between you and his golf/football/cars/fishing. There's time for all of you!

1-800-ROMANCE

1

*A*uthentic, signed photographs of your favorite movie stars! Call Autographed Collectibles at 800-382-3075.

2

G IANT BANNERS, from Supergram, at 800-3-BANNER.

3

*C*ustom-made jigsaw puzzles from Bits & Pieces: 800-JIGSAWS.

4

800-284-JAVA…will get you coffee delivered to your doorstep.

The essence of romance is communication.

5

A 50-page catalog of romantic gifts! "Marketplace" is full of specially chosen items for romantics. Call 800-642-7462.

6

*H*ow about a Caribbean vacation at an all-inclusive luxury resort for couples only?! Call 800-SANDALS.

Romantic Resources

1

*H*ow about a free subscription to the Love-Letter—"The newsletter of romantic ideas"?! Send your name and address to:

> LoveLetter
> P.O. Box 372
> Naperville, IL   60566

2

*H*ow about an elegant, custom-made greeting card for your honey? Your favorite verse or quote will be rendered in calligraphy, and then decorated with a hand-painted flower. Around $50. Call Pendragon Ink at 508-234-6843.

Passive people never live
passionate lives.

3
. . .

$\mathscr{J}$im Rickert, "The Songsmith" will write and record original love songs for you! Customized with your names; available in any style (rock, country, ballad, etc.) and recorded on cassette tape! Call Jim at 617-471-8800.

4
. . .

$\mathscr{M}$arriage Magazine—Celebrating the Potential of Marriage. A spin-off from the well-respected

Marriage Encounter organization, *Marriage* is not a religious magazine, but one that does include spirituality among the mix of relationship issues that confront us all. Call for a subscription: 800-MARRIAGE.

5

*S*ome gift catalogs:

- ❧ The Smithsonian: 800-322-0344
- ❧ Golf House: 800-336-4446
- ❧ Neiman Marcus: 800-825-8000
- ❧ Anyone Can Whistle: 800-435-8863
- ❧ Sporty's: 800-543-8633
- ❧ Sundance: 800-422-2770
- ❧ The Nature Company: 800-227-1114

Happy Birthday!

1
. . .

*G*et her a wedding cake instead of a birthday cake!

2
. . .

*P*ut sparklers instead of candles on his birthday cake! Celebrate your similarities. Honor your differences.

3
. . .

*C*elebrate your partner's "Half-Birthday" (the date exactly six months from his or her actual birthday)!

4
. . .

*G*et her an actual newspaper from the day she was born! Call The Historic Newspaper Archives at 800-221-3221.

𝒮end him one birthday card for each year of his age—one-a-day for as long as it takes. Or...send him one birthday card for each year of his age—all at one time!

Be My Valentine

1
. . .

𝐵uy two Valentine's cards. Send one for Valentine's Day, and send the other one in August!

2
. . .

𝒞elebrate Valentine's Day 365 days a year!

———

The anticipation is often just as much fun as the event or gift itself.

———

*Y*ou can get your Valentine card specially post-marked from Loveland, Colorado! Just put your card and stamped envelope, addressed to your love, inside another envelope addressed to: Postmaster, Loveland, Colorado 80537.

Musical Interludes

1

. . .

*H*ave his favorite song—or "Your Song"—playing on the stereo when he returns home from work.

2

. . .

*R*omance for the musically inclined: Write out a few bars of the musical score of a lovesong. Send it to your partner without a title and without the words. The challenge is for him or her to figure-out what song it is.

Some recommendations for your Romantic Music Library:

- *Barefoot Ballet*, a romantic CD by John Klemmer.
- *Living Inside Your Love*, the CD by George Benson
- *Openings*, the CD by William Ellwood
- *Forever Friends*, the CD by Justo Almario

Romantic Miscellany

1
. . .

Get the pizza chef to arrange the pepperoni in the shape of a heart.

2
. . .

Put a tiny love note inside a ballon, then attach a pin to the string.

3

*V*isit Love, Arizona; Bliss, New York; Valentine, Montana; Loving, Nebraska; or Loveland, Colorado.

Romantic Potpourri

1

*H*ide 25 little love notes all over the house.

2

*B*ook a three-day weekend at a romantic bed & breakfast.

3

*G*o on a picnic...in your living room...at work...at midnight...on a Tuesday afternoon...

Turn the ordinary into the special.

4
. . .

A weekend without TV. A day without the kids. An evening without interruptions.

Help for the Hopeless

1
. . .

Change something in your routine. Get up an hour early and enjoy a leisurely breakfast together. Quit work at noon!

2
. . .

Create a "Stay-In-Touch Kit." Contents include pen, paper, envelopes (pre-addressed), love stamps, a list of suggestions for what to write, a photo of you with a funny caption, directions to the post office, etc.

Romance is a state of mind.

3

*U*se your Scrabble game to leave each other cryptic love notes!

Hope for the Helpless

1

*P*ropose a toast. Take a walk. Go for a ride. Sleep in late. Write a note. Pen a poem. Sing a song.

2

*O*ne way to generate romantic ideas is to focus on your partner. If you focus your attention on her—just think about her a little more often—then romantic ideas will simply pop-up all around you!

I guarantee it. Romantic gifts will jump off store shelves into your hands, and romantic opportunities will present themselves to you unbidden.

3

*W*hen traveling, give your partner one rose for each day you'll be away.

4

*P*lay hookey from work. Stay home together. Sleep in late. Make lazy love. Catch a movie matinee.

Movie Madness

1

*H*ow about some classic romantic movies starring some of the all-time great romantic couples:

- *Red Dust* (Gable & Harlow)
- *Hold Your Man* (Gable & Harlow)

- *Flying Down to Rio* (Astaire & Rogers)
- *Top Hat* (Astaire & Rogers)
- *Maytime* (MacDonald & Eddy)
- *Sweethearts* (MacDonald & Eddy)
- *Love Finds Andy Hardy* (Garland & Rooney)
- *Girl Crazy* (Garland & Rooney)
- *That Forsyte Woman* (Garson & Pidgeon)
- *Scandal at Scourie* (Garson & Pidgeon)
- *To Have and Have Not* (Bogart & Bacall)
- *Key Largo* (Bogart & Bacall)
- *Fire Over England* (Leigh & Olivier)
- *21 Days Together* (Leigh & Olivier)
- *Cleopatra* (Taylor & Burton)
- *The Sandpiper* (Taylor & Burton)
- *The Long, Hot Summer* (Newman & Woodward)
- *Paris Blues* (Newman & Woodward)
- *Woman of the Year* (Hepburn & Tracy)
- *Without Love* (Hepburn & Tracy)

2

And some current romantic movies:

- ❧ *Somewhere in Time*
- ❧ *Out of Africa*
- ❧ *When Harry Met Sally*
- ❧ *Ghost*
- ❧ *An Officer and a Gentleman*
- ❧ *On Golden Pond*
- ❧ *Beauty and the Beast*
- ❧ *Splash*
- ❧ *The Accidental Tourist*
- ❧ *The Way We Were*
- ❧ *Sleepless In Seattle*

For Singles Only

1
. . .

*M*ail her a copy of your resume instead of a greeting card. Attach a note: "I'd like you to get to know me better."

2
. . .

*H*ow do you know when to "get serious"? When intimacy becomes more important than excitement.

———

Money can't buy you love...but it can buy you a little romance!

———

3
. . .

*C*reate and fill-out an application for the "job" of "Boyfriend" or "Girlfriend."

$\mathcal{G}$als: Send flowers to him.

5
· · ·

$\mathcal{G}$uys: Send her a fruit basket. Attach notes to each item: "You're the apple of my eye." "You're a peach!" "I'm going bananas over you!"

For Marrieds Only

1
· · ·

$\mathcal{Y}$ou've heard it said that "There are no guarantees in life." That's true. But you just may be able to get a Warranty. Here's what one guy did: At the conclusion of his marriage ceremony, he presented his new wife with a "Lifetime Relationship Warranty"!

The Playful Side of Love

2

Renew your wedding vows. Create a private ceremony just for the two of you.

3

Go on a second (third, fourth, fifth, sixth!) honeymoon.

4

Visit the place where you first met; where you went on your first date; where you had your first kiss; where you got married...

5

"Happy 100th Anniversary—99 years in advance!" (A card from newlywed Suzie B. to very surprised husband David.)

6

*H*ave your wedding vows rendered in beautiful calligraphy, frame them and hang them on the living room wall.

7

*G*et a vintage wine from the year of your anniversary.

Mindset of a Romantic

1

*T*ry "Couple-Thinking"—viewing yourself first as a member of a couple. This doesn't mean ignoring yourself, but it does mean that you keep your relationship in first place.

2

$\mathcal{R}$omance is a process—it's not an event. It's not a one-time thing. It's not something that's "accomplished," and then forgotten. In order to work, it's got to be an ongoing thing—a part of the very fabric of your daily life.

3

$\mathcal{G}$o above and beyond. Do the unexpected. Give more than you have to.

If you change attitudes you always influence behavior. If you change behavior you only sometimes change attitudes.

4

*T*he Golden Rule doesn't always work! "Do unto others as you would have them do unto you" would lead clothes-lovers to buy their partners outfits; workaholics to buy their partners briefcases; and handymen to buy their wives tools! Try The Platinum Rule: "Do unto others as they want to be done unto." Think about it.

Romance on a Budget

1

*O*n her birthday, send her mother a Thank You card.

2

*G*iftwrap a wishbone in a jewelry box. Send it to your lover with a note that says, "I wish you were here."

3

$\mathcal{A}$ picnic in the park.

4

$\mathcal{P}$icking a bouquet of wildflowers.

Creative Gift Ideas

1

$\mathcal{B}$uy one blue gift and three red ones…two small gifts and one big one…three $5 gifts and one $25 gift.

2

$\mathcal{G}$et every recording ever made by his favorite musical group.

3

$\mathcal{G}$et every book ever written by her favorite author.

Romantic Mischief

4
. . .

*H*e gave her a simple little music box that plays *As Time Goes By*. As she opened it, he said to her, "As time goes by I love you more and more."

She gave him the key to her apartment in a jewelry box. As he opened it, she said, "It's the key to my heart, too. You've unlocked it—please don't break it."

The real gift in each case was what was said in conjunction with the gift. Think about it!

5
. . .

*C*reate "theme gifts" based on his/her favorite music, color, cartoon, flower, TV show, snack food, season or hobby.

Romantic gestures have no ulterior motive. Their only purpose is to express love.

6
. . .

$\mathscr{B}$ouquets of flowers are fine…but creative romantics have reported…

- ✧ Homemade bouquets of cookies.
- ✧ Homemade bouquets of $10 bills.
- ✧ Homemade bouquets of tea bags.

Little Gestures

1
. . .

$\mathscr{L}$ittle gestures can communicate volumes. A look, a raised eyebrow, a touch on the elbow, the smallest hints of body language, can communicate volumes between two lovers who are in-tune with one another. Intimacy is built on such small things.

2
. . .

$\mathscr{C}$ollect quotes on love. Write each one on a 3x5 card. When you've collected a hundred or so, begin a Campaign of Love by mailing them, posting them, hiding them and showering them on your lover.

3

$\mathcal{H}$ey, you guys, write her a love letter! It doesn't have to be perfect, poetic, long or particularly eloquent. Just put your feelings on paper.

4

$\mathcal{W}$ords that men love to hear:

- ✤ "I believe in you."
- ✤ "I want you."
- ✤ "You're the greatest."

5

$\mathcal{W}$ords that women love to hear:

- ✤ "I cherish you."
- ✤ "I need you."
- ✤ "I adore you."

For Singles Only, Part II

"Think Like a Married Person: Strategy #1"

Intimacy

Although you can't force intimacy, you can make it a goal. When you think about it, many goals of single folks are short-term at best, and downright shallow at worst: relieving loneliness, "scoring," finding a great dance partner.

If, instead, intimacy is your goal, you'll share more of yourself sooner, you'll communicate honestly, and you'll listen to the other more attentively.

"Think Like a Married Person: Strategy #2"

Long-term thinking

The single brain is consumed with short-term

goals: this Friday night, this Saturday night, what will I wear?—Will he kiss me tonight?—Will she sleep with me on the second date? Chill-out, singles!

A long-term mindset will relieve a lot of your stress, help you be more "yourself," and give you a better perspective on things.

3

"Think Like a Married Person: Strategy #3"

Communicating

*H*ave you ever noticed that single people often do a lot of talking without really communicating much? The singles scene is often characterized by a lot of posturing, boasting and clever bantering.

Those who get beyond these things the most quickly tend to end up in the best relationships.

For Marrieds Only, Part II

1
. . .

"Think Like a Single Person: Strategy #1"

Flirting

*W*hen's the last time you actually flirted with your own husband (or wife)? Try it the next time you're out at a party together. (Don't be surprised if your spouse wants to leave the party early!)

2
. . .

"Think Like a Single Person: Strategy #2"

Instant gratification

*T*he typical mindset of a married person is long-term. The positive side of this is that long-term can mean security, commitment and comfort; the negative side is that it can also mean boredom, laziness and non-activity.

One way to combat this negative side is to adopt the mindset of a single person: It's a mindset of instant gratification. Horny? Make love now. Thinking of her? Call her now. Appreciate him? Hug him now.

3
. . .

"Think Like a Single Person: Strategy #3"

Seduction

*W*hen's the last time you seduced your spouse? How often do you bother to "set the mood," play the music, dress the part, say the right words, do the little things?

Love Songs, Part II

1
. . .

*R*omantic duets...You could sing them in harmony together...Or write the lyrics in a love note...Or record a favorite song on a cassette tape and give it to your partner in a Walkman.

- *Almost Paradise*, Reno & Wilson
- *Always,* Atlantic Starr
- *Don't Know Much*, Ronstadt & Neville
- *I Got You Babe*, Sonny & Cher
- *Islands in the Stream*, Parton & Rogers
- *Love Makes Things Happen*, Pebbles & Babyface
- *Nothing's Gonna Stop Us Now*, Starship
- *Opposites Attract*, Paula Abdul & MC Skat Cat
- *Somewhere Out There*, Ronstadt & Ingram
- *Time of My Life*, Medley & Warnes

2

*A*nd some other romantic favorites…

- *Shelter of My Love*, Jimmy Cliff

- *I'll Always Love You*, Tayler Dayne
- *True Love*, Bing Crosby
- *Suddenly*, Billy Ocean
- *Take My Breath Away*, Berlin
- *Rambling Rose*, Nat King Cole
- *I (Who Have Nothing)*, Tom Jones
- *In Your Eyes*, Peter Gabriel
- *You're My World*, Helen Reddy
- *To Be With You*, Mister Big
- *Time In a Bottle*, Jim Croce
- *Dream On*, Oak Ridge Boys
- *Wonderful Tonight*, Eric Clapton
- *Overjoyed*, Stevie Wonder
- *Have I Told You Lately That I Love You*, Van Morrison
- *Evergreen*, Barbra Streisand
- *Lady*, Kenny Rogers

*H*ave the lyrics from a favorite song rendered in calligraphy and framed.

Love Letters

1

*W*rite a love letter. Cut the paper into puzzle-shaped pieces. Mail the pieces to your lover…one piece per day!

2

*I*nclude some pressed flowers inside the envelope, along with your love letter.

3

I don't need to remind you, do I, that love letters should be stamped with special Love Stamps from the post office?! I didn't think so.

Romance is the process...
Love is the goal.

4
. . .

$\mathcal{W}$rite a "Stream-of-Consciousness" Love Letter.
Just sit down and start writing...whatever comes to
mind about your partner...your feelings and
hopes...memories and dreams.

5
. . .

$\mathcal{I}$f you're not much of a writer, you could compose an audio love letter!

6
. . .

$\mathcal{S}$end a love letter scented with your cologne or
perfume.

Taking Care of Business

1

. . .

*O*ne couple created a "Romance Credit Card." Here's how it works: They created their own "bank" which issues two types of credit: money and time.

On a quarterly basis the "bank officers" meet to establish their credit limits. When cash is tight, they provide for more time. They keep their credit card balances on a chart on the refrigerator, and they each carry a "Romance Credit Card" in their wallets as a reminder that they have an obligation to spend a little time and money on their relationship on a regular basis.

2

. . .

*D*o you want him to call you more often? Try leaving subtle hints, like hundreds of Post-It Notes with your phone number stuck all over the place: in his briefcase, on the underside of the toilet lid, in his desk drawers at work, in his calendar, in the medicine chest, on his steering wheel, on the lawnmower, on the front door, on his pillow, in his socks...

Weird & Wild

1
. . .

*T*ake some favorite photo, attach "cartoon balloons" to them and mail them to him at work.

2
. . .

*T*ie a piece of string to the inside doorknob of your front door. String it throughout the house, tracing a path that leads to the bathtub; be in it waiting for your lover.

Great relationships aren't 50/50—
they're 100/100.

The Playful Side of Love

3
. . .

*A*nd then, of course, there's always the umbrella-
built-for-two!

4
. . .

*H*alf a tattoo is better than one (I think...!)
Christine and Matthew M., of Topeka, Kansas,
each got half a heart tattooed on their forearms.
When they press their arms together, they form
one complete heart!

Little Things Mean a Lot

1
. . .

*A*lways kiss each other upon departing.

2
. . .

*B*rush her hair for her.

3

*H*ave you ever tried to buy a heart-shaped box at any time of the year other than Valentine's Day? It's nearly impossible to find one! The solution? Stock up on them early in February! Great for wrapping romantic surprises year-round!

4

A wintertime bath suggestion. Warm her towel in the dryer!

5

*S*ave some mistletoe from Christmas—and use it in July!

Yikes!

1

*K*eep a bulletin board for tacking-up love notes, ticket stubs and other mementos. (One couple had a bulletin board that overflowed and eventually took over an entire room!)

2

*O*ne pair of wine afficionados wallpapered a room with wine labels!

3

*U*se more than one sense in your romantic communications. Because our sense of smell is our most under-utilized sense, here are some ways of adding some sensuous aromas to your lover's life:

- Don't just buy any old bouquet of flowers—ask your florist to suggest some especially fragrant flowers. Here's a start: freesia, lilacs, stock, gardenias, Casablanca lilies, Rubrum lilies and stephanotis.

- Don't just hide some lingerie in his briefcase—add a dash of his favorite perfume.

- Perfume his pillow as a signal that you want to make love tonight.

You Must Remember This

1
. . .

*H*ow many minutes per day of undivided attention do you give your lover?

2
. . .

*H*ave you been receiving your M.D.R.R.? (Minimum Daily Requirement of Romance.) How much romance do you want and need in your life? How much do you want daily—weekly—monthly—yearly? How does this compare with your partner's wants and needs?

Celebrate without reason.
Give without strings. Love without
stopping. Feel without fear.
Dance without music.

Number a sheet of paper from 1 to 100, and title it "100 Reasons Why I Love You." Complete the list over the next week.

Another list: "100 Places Where I'd Like to Make Love With You."

A Kiss Is Just a Kiss

1

Compose a love poem together. You write one verse, she writes the next. Work on it for an hour...or over the course of a week...a month...a year...a lifetime!

2

Gary G. gets his romantic exercise by stealing street signs that contain his wife's name! He says he has quite a collection from cities and villages across the U.S.A. (I'm not endorsing this kind of heinous behavior, of course. But it is a pretty cool idea, don't you think?!)

3
. . .

*I*f your mother told you not to play with your food, then your mother wasn't much of a romantic. Here's a recipe for romance:

Make some toast. Carefully carve-out a heart in the middle. Set the toast in a frying pan. Fry an egg in the heart-shaped hole. Serve to your lover. Voila!—A romantic breakfast!

Outrageous!

1
. . .

*T*hrow-out your TV: It will create more time for you to share with each other.

2

$\mathscr{A}$ one-hour, no-limit shopping spree in her favorite mall. (On your mark, get set, go!)

3

$\mathscr{A}$ gift certificate to Tiffany's.

4

$\mathscr{D}$inner in each of the finest restaurants in America.

5

$\mathscr{W}$ear a tuxedo home from work…just for the heck of it!

Around the House

1

$\mathscr{I}$magine your bedroom filled with helium balloons.

2

*I*magine making love on the dining room table.

3

*I*magine picnicking in the den in front of the fireplace.

4

*I*magine a (quiet) weekend with the kids away at camp.

5

*I*magine the bathtub filled with Hershey's Kisses.

6

*I*magine a bubblebath together...with the bathroom filled with candles (like in that awesome scene from the movie *Bull Durham*).

Flower Power

1

"*The* Perpetual Bouquet": Bring home one flower a day. You'll build a wonderfully diverse bouquet day-by-day.

2

*P*lace a flower under the windshield of his car.

3

*S*pread rose pedals on your bed...or float them in a hot bubblebath.

4

*E*dible flowers! Tiger lilies, zucchini flowers, nasturtiums, calendulas, Johnny jump-ups, lemon-scented marigolds, pineapple sage and rose geraniums.

5

$\mathcal{T}$ake that extra step and create a flower arrangement that has symbolic significance. Christa Cragg, for instance, once sent eleven red roses and one white rose. The note, of course, said, "You're one-of-a-kind!"

6

$\mathcal{D}$on't simply send flowers…Make your flowers into a meaningful and symbolic gift. Give some special thought to your note: "The white freesia symbolize the light you've brought into my life. The yellow daffodils remind me of the gold in our wedding rings. The red roses symbolize the bloom of our love."

Erotica

1

$\mathcal{G}$uys: Get her some really elegant lingerie. (Not that outrageous stuff you prefer.)

Gals: Get yourself some really outrageous lingerie. (Not that elegant stuff you prefer.)

2

*H*ave you ever covered a portion of your lover's body with food, and then licked it off?

3

*E*rotic fiction, humbly submitted for your perusal:

- *Tart Tales*—Elegant Erotic Stories, by Carolyn Banks
- *My Secret Garden*, by Nancy Friday
- *Forbidden Flowers*, also by Nancy Friday
- *Women on Top*, by…Nancy Friday
- *The Unbearable Lightness of Being*, by Milan Kundera

$\mathcal{E}$ach month, subtly focus on a different part of her body. Give her massages, stroke her, buy her little gifts for that part of her body. See how long it takes her to notice!

ABCs of Love

$\mathcal{A}$lways kiss each other upon departing.

$\mathcal{B}$e there for her. Always.

$\mathcal{C}$reate an environment of love.

$\mathcal{D}$o it. Now.

$\mathcal{E}$scape from the kids.

$\mathcal{F}$ight fair.

$\mathcal{G}$ive of your time.

$\mathcal{H}$andle with care.

Inspire your partner with your love.

Judge not.

Keep your good memories alive.

Listen to her.

Make love with your partner's needs foremost.

Never go to bed mad.

Offer to handle an unpleasant chore.

Praise him.

Quality time isn't just for the kids.

Respect her feelings.

Say what you feel when you feel it.

Tell her you love her every day. Every day. Every day. Every day.

Understand your differences.

Valentine's Day is every day.

$\mathcal{W}$alk together. Talk together.

E$\mathcal{X}$cite your partner as only you know how.

$\mathcal{Y}$ou can never say "I love you" too often.

$\mathcal{Z}$ero-in on his little passions.

More Romantic Resources

1

$\mathcal{D}$o you like sexy shoes? Well, there's a catalog called "Sexy Shoes"—just for you. Call 'em at 517-734-4030.

2

$\mathcal{H}$ow about an original, signed photograph of your honey's hero, favorite movie star or celebrity?

"Recollections" has thousands of them! Call for a catalog: 908-747-3858.

3
. . .

*F*or your loving lawyer, "For Counsel," a whole darn catalog full of stuff for lawyers! Call 800-637-0098.

4
. . .

*H*ow about a personalized board game based on the two of you? Includes illustrations and custom trivia cards. Cool! Call "Anyone's Game" at 800-448-5431.

5
. . .

*F*or the pilot or aviation nut: The "Tailwinds" catalog, with aviation clothing, authentic flight jackets, jewelry, etc. Call 800-992-7737.

Romantic Reminders

1
. . .

$\mathscr{P}$lace a heart-shaped sticker on the face of your watch. It's a reminder to call your partner during the day.

2
. . .

$\mathscr{W}$rite little love notes on your honey's calendar. Write notes on dates that are months away.

3
. . .

$\mathscr{C}$reate little "coded messages" that you can write to you partner that no one else will be able to understand. Some examples:

- ❦ Y.A.M.O.A.O.—"You are my one and only."

- ❦ L.M.L.T.—"Let's make love tonight."

- ❦ Y.A.M.S.—"You are my sweetie."

Romantic Thoughts

1

*N*ot that it matters, but I was just thinking...Why do we have birthday cakes and wedding cakes, but no anniversary cakes or Valentine cakes?

2

*N*ot that it matters, but I was just thinking...Why do we have Christmas tree ornaments, but no special ornaments with which to celebrate other special occasions?

3

*N*ot that it matters, but I was just thinking...Why is Columbus Day a national holiday, and Valentine's Day isn't?

Kinda Crazy

1

❧ The item: A bottle of tabasco sauce.

❧ The note: "You're hot stuff!"

2

❧ The item: A bar of Caress soap.

❧ The note: "I'm going to Caress you in the tub tonight!"

3

❧ The item: A bottle of Joy dishwashing liquid.

❧ The note: "You are the Joy of my life."

❦ The item: A lottery ticket.

❦ The note: "I hit the jackpot when I found you."

Little Things

*G*et a little bottle. (Maybe an antique bottle or a medicine bottle.) Fill it with sand. Cork it. Label it: "Extra Time." Give it to your partner.

*S*ave your partner one minute of time.

❦ Wipe the snow from her windshield.

❦ Open the newspaper to his favorite section.

❦ Get up a few minutes early to start the coffee.

3
. . .

$\mathcal{S}$hare something.

❧ A cup of tea.

❧ A glass of wine.

❧ A good joke.

4
. . .

$\mathcal{P}$amper your partner.

❧ Brush her hair.

❧ Give him a foot massage.

❧ Give her the TV remote control.

Musical Messages

1
. . .

$\mathcal{S}$ongs to help you express your feelings.
Friendship & Appreciation:

- *That's What Friends Are For*, Dionne Warwick
- *Bridge Over Troubled Waters,* Simon & Garfunkel
- *Thank You for Being a Friend*, Andrew Gold
- *You've Got a Friend*, James Taylor (and Carole King, too)
- *Stand By Me*, Ben E. King

Compile a custom cassette tape of songs for your honey.

2

Songs to help you express your feelings. Desire & Sexual Attraction:

- *Sexual Healing*, Marvin Gaye
- *Feel Like Makin' Love*, Bad Company
- *I Want Your Sex*, George Michael
- *Afternoon Delight*, Starland Vocal Band
- *Let's Spend the Night Together*, Rolling Stones

✿ *Natural Woman*, Aretha Franklin

*U*se some of these songs to get your partner "in the mood."

3

*S*ongs to help you express your feelings. Loneliness & Missing You:

✿ *Wishing You Were Here*, Chicago

✿ *Far Away*, Carole King

✿ *Missing You*, Jim Reeves

✿ *I Miss You Like Crazy*, Natalie Cole

✿ *Missing You Now*, Michael Bolton

*W*hen you or your partner are going away on a trip, give him or her a cassette tape with some of these songs. Pack it along with a Walkman!

4

Songs to help you express your feelings.
Anniversary & Celebrations:

- *Always and Forever*, Heatwave
- *Forever and Ever, Amen*, Randy Travis
- *Our Love Is Here to Stay*, Harry Connick, Jr.
- *The Anniversary Song*, Richard Tucker
- *More Today Than Yesterday*, Spiral Staircase

Get a CD changer that plays several different CDs. Program it to play your preselected songs.

5

Songs to help you express your feelings. Love & Tenderness:

- *Lady*, Kenny Rogers
- *Endless Love*, Diana Ross
- *Always On My Mind*, Willie Nelson

- *Just the Way You Are*, Billy Joel
- *I Honestly Love You*, Olivia Newton John
- *You Are So Beautiful (To Me)*, Joe Cocker
- *Through the Years*, Kenny Rogers
- *Longer Than*, Dan Fogelberg
- *Evergreen*, Barbra Streisand

*B*e careful with these songs. They may induce tears.

6
. . .

*S*ongs to help you express your feelings. Intense Love:

- *When A Man Loves a Woman*, Percy Sledge
- *Crazy For You*, Madonna
- *Wind Beneath My Wings*, Bette Midler
- *Closer to Believing*, Emerson, Lake & Palmer
- *I Am Waiting*, Yes

❧ *I Will Always Love You*, Whitney Houston

❧ *Nights In White Satin*, Moody Blues

WARNING: Intense feelings bursting out all over the place!

7

···

$\mathcal{S}$ongs to help you express your feelings. Love & Joy:

❧ *Love Me Do*, Beatles

❧ *I Just Called to Say I Love You*, Stevie Wonder

❧ *You Are the Sunshine of My Life*, Stevie Wonder

❧ *The Way You Do the Things You Do*, Temptations

❧ *What a Wonderful World*, Louis Armstrong

❧ *It Had to Be You*, Harry Connick, Jr.

❧ *How Sweet It Is*, James Taylor

$\mathcal{C}$reate a custom cassette tape. Put it in the tape player in her car. Set it to start playing as soon as the car starts up.

Fun, Fun, Fun!

1
. . .

$\mathcal{G}$et a vanity license plate for your car with your honey's name on it.

2
. . .

$\mathcal{C}$reate a vanity license plate that includes as "secret message"—for example:

- ✺ YAM-LFE   "You And Me—Lovers For Ever"
- ✺ WTAO   "We Two Are One"
- ✺ ILY-MTTY   "I Love You More Today Than Yesterday"

Collection of Catalogs

1.
. . .

$\mathcal{G}$ifts for the movie buff...can be found in Rick's Movie Graphics Catalog. Call 800-252-0425.

2

$\mathcal{G}$ifts for the playboy in your life...can be found in the Playboy Catalog. Call 800-423-9494.

3

$\mathcal{G}$ifts for all seasons...can be found in the Seasons Catalog. Call 800-776-9677.

4

$\mathcal{G}$ifts for the game lover...can be found in the Worldwide Games Catalog. Call 800-888-0987.

5

$\mathcal{G}$ifts with attitude...can be found in the Attitudes Catalog. Call 800-525-2468.

Big Stuff

1

*H*ire a skywriter to write a love message in the sky for you!

2

*P*lan a surprise vacation. Pack suitcases for both of you; arrange for your partner to get time off work; make all the arrangements ahead of time. Then simply drive your honey to the airport and take off together!

3

*C*reate a huge "I LOVE YOU" banner—drape it over the front of your house.

4

*M*ake a ten-foot-tall anniversary card.

5

*W*rite "I LOVE YOU" on your driveway with colored chalk.

Little Stuff

1

A little gold locket with your photo inside.

2

*C*arving your initials in a tree.

3

*I*nscribing your initials in wet cement on a sidewalk.

4

*M*ake "I love you" the first words out of your mouth every morning, and the last words you speak every night.

Romantic Mischief

Love Letters, Part II

1

*W*rite a love letter that recalls how you first fell in love with your partner.

2

*W*rite a love letter that describes the reasons why you're committed to your partner and your relationship.

3

*W*rite a love letter that is subtlely seductive and erotic.

4

*W*rite a love letter that is blatantly steamy and sexy.

Gifts vs. Presents

1

$\mathcal{D}$o you know what the difference between a "gift" and a "present" is? A gift is something that the receiver wants. A present is something that the giver wants the receiver to have.

2

$\mathcal{W}$hen a man gives a woman lingerie—guess what?!—nine times out of ten it's a present. When he gives her favorite perfume, it's a gift. When a woman gives a man a necktie it's usually a present. When she gives him a new golf club, it's a gift.

3

$\mathcal{T}$his is not to say that one is better than the other. Gifts and presents are just different. Gifts say more about the receiver: You've listened to your partner. Presents say more about the giver: They express your feelings.

$\mathcal{K}$nowing the difference between a gift and a present will help both of you stay in-tune with each other and avoid unrealistic expectations and possible hard feelings. Note: Items can sometimes be both gifts and presents at the same time.

Just Do It!

1

$\mathcal{C}$reate a new mixed drink and name it after your lover.

2

$\mathcal{W}$rite the "Longest Love Letter in History": Write one paragraph per day, every day, for a solid year—then wrap it up and mail it to your lover.

3

*B*ake a batch of (heart-shaped) chocolate chip cookies.

4

A gentle touch. A simple gesture. A kind word. A wink of an eye.

Q&A

1

*A*re you a business executive? Create a "Love Plan" based on a business plan. Now implement it!

2

*A*re you a secretary? Write a love note in the style of an inter-office memo.

3

*A*re you a gardener? Find ways to weed-out the negative in your relationship, and shower your partner with love.

4

*A*re you a teacher? Write a "Relationship Curriculum." Grade yourselves at the end of the semester.

5

*A*re you a mechanic? How could you "tune-up" your relationship?

Guys and Gals

1

*G*uys: Revive gallantry. Open doors for her. Carry packages for her. Help her on with her coat.

2

*G*als: Send a balloon bouquet to him at work.

3

*G*uys: Here's the correct way to kiss a woman's hand: You hold her hand and lower your head to kiss her hand—you don't raise her hand to your lips!

4

*G*als: Create a custom cassette tape of you singing his favorite song.

Things You Probably Never Thought Of

1

*C*reate a new flavor of ice cream by mixing together different flavors of ice cream and different candy or chocolate or whatever...pack it into an empty Ben & Jerry's container...name the flavor after your partner...create a new label for the container...and present it to your ice cream loving lover!

2

Create a "This Is Your Life" videotape for your partner by interviewing his or her parents, brothers and sisters, relatives, friends, teachers and associates.

3

Create a multi-part "Theme Gift": Wrap these items separately, then place all of them into one large box: a copy of *The Joy of Sex*; a copy of *The Joy of Cooking*; a new set of pots and pans; and some sexy lingerie.

4

You don't have to be eloquent in order to be romantic! You can let other people speak for you!

Borrow some timeless words from William Shakespeare, Billy Joel, Paul McCartney, Charlie Brown, Susan Polis Schutz, Elizabeth Barrett Browning, Kahlil Gibran.

Overdo It!

1

Get every recording ever made by his favorite musical group.

2

Get every book ever written by her favorite author.

3

Rent every movie starring his favorite actor.

4

Get 25 pounds of her favorite candy.

5

Give her ten dozen red roses on Valentine's Day.

Avoid Generic Gifts

1

Find obscure recordings by her favorite singer.

2

Get him season tickets for his favorite sports team.

3

Wrap all her gifts in her favorite color.

4

Get him a book signed by his favorite author.

5

$\mathscr{G}$et her a movie poster from her favorite film.

Shopping Tips

1

$\mathscr{B}$uy one blue gift, two red gifts, and one green gift.

2

$\mathscr{F}$ind two gifts for under $5, three gifts for $20-$25, and one gift for $50-$100.

3

$\mathscr{G}$et two sentimental gifts, one gag gift, and one practical gift.

4

*G*et one gift in a toy store, one in a hardware store, and one in a grocery store.

5

*G*et one gift that will appeal to her mind, one gift that will please her sense of beauty, and one gift that will stimulate her sexually.

Love Stories

1

*H*er husband was a handyman. He loved to take things apart and put them back together again. She gave him a fancy VCR for his birthday...she took it apart and gave it to him wrapped in sixteen different boxes!

2

$\mathcal{H}$e gave her a gift for no special occasion. A beautifully wrapped box from Tiffany's! She opened it to find a sterling silver tray—engraved with "Sally, will you marry me?"

3

$\mathcal{S}$he loved "shoe string licorice." He wrote her a message in licorice letters one day: "Love ya, babe." She ate it up.

4

$\mathcal{S}$he loved flowers. On their first anniversary, he gave her one rose; on their second anniversary, two roses; on their third, three. They've been married 52 years now.

Musical Magic

*R*omantic background music? Glad you asked...

- Tom Scott
- George Benson
- Natalie Cole
- Kenny G
- David Lanz
- William Ackerman
- David Benoit
- Harry Connick, Jr.
- George Winston
- Billie Holiday
- Stan Getz
- Andreas Vollenweider
- Grover Washington, Jr.

- Richard Clayderman
- Yanni
- Enya
- David Sanborn
- Earl Klugh
- Liz Story
- Luther Vandross
- Larry Carlton

A Daily Romantic Checklist

- Compliment your partner.
- Spend twenty minutes of uninterrupted time together.
- Check-in with each other during the day.
- Perform one small—and unexpected—gesture.
- Say "I love you" at least three times.

- Thank your partner for something.
- Look for romantic concepts in the newspaper.
- Take an extra minute when kissing good-bye.

A Weekly Romantic Checklist

- Bring home one small, unexpected gift or present.
- Share some form of physical intimacy.
- Share an entire afternoon or evening together.
- Share two insights you gained this week.
- Write at least one little love note.
- Mail something to your partner.
- Plan something special for the upcoming weekend.

A Monthly Romantic Checklist

꙳ Plan one romantic surprise for this month.

꙳ Restock your stash of greeting cards.

꙳ Go out to dinner once or twice.

꙳ Rent at least two romantic movies.

꙳ Make love!

꙳ Make plans for a romantic weekend sometime soon.

꙳ Plan one romantic event with a seasonal theme.

Romantic Mischief

A Yearly Romantic Checklist

- ❧ Make a New Year's resolution to be a more creative romantic.

- ❧ Make plans for your next anniversary.

- ❧ Think of an unusual way to celebrate your partner's birthday.

- ❧ Review your plans for your next vacation.

- ❧ Create a special "Romance" category in your household budget.

- ❧ Make plans for Valentine's Day—well in advance!

For a free one-year subscription to Greg Godek's *LoveLetter Newsletter* send your name and address to:

LoveLetter
Sourcebooks
P.O. Box 372
Naperville, IL 60566

Would you like to see your name in print in a future book?! If you have a romantic, creative or outrageous story that you would like to share, please send it to:

Love Stories
Sourcebooks
P.O. Box 372
Naperville, IL 60566

Would you be interested in having Greg Godek present a speech or seminar to your group? For more information, please call his office at:

630-961-3900

Other books in this series include:

Romantic Dates: Ways to Woo & Wow the One You Love
ISBN: 1-57071-153-4; $6.95

Romantic Fantasies: & Other Sexy Ways of Expressing Your Love
ISBN: 1-57071-154-2; $6.95

Romantic Questions: Growing Closer Through
Intimate Conversation
ISBN: 1-57071-152-6; $6.95

Also by Gregory J.P. Godek

1001 Ways to Be Romantic
5th Anniversary Edition of the Bestselling Classic!
ISBN: 1-883518-05-9; $14.95

1001 More Ways to Be Romantic
ISBN: 0-9629803-2-3; $11.95

To order these books or any other of our many publications, please
contact your local bookseller, gift store or call Sourcebooks. Books
by Gregory J.P. Godek are available in book and gift stores across
North America. Get a copy of our catalog by writing or faxing:

Sourcebooks
P. O. Box 372
Naperville, IL 60566
(630) 961-3900
FAX: (630) 961-2168